World Wisdom
The Library of Perennial Philosophy

The Library of Perennial Philosophy is dedicated to the exposition of the timeless Truth underlying the diverse religions. This Truth, often referred to as the *Sophia Perennis*—or Perennial Wisdom—finds its expression in the revealed Scriptures as well as the writings of the great sages and the artistic creations of the traditional worlds.

Native Spirit: The Sun Dance Way appears as one of our selections in the Treasures of the World's Religions series.

Treasures of the World's Religions Series

This series of anthologies presents scriptures and the writings of the great spiritual authorities of the past on fundamental themes. Some titles are dovoted to a single spiritual tradition, while others have a unifying topic that touches upon traditions from both the East and West, such as prayer and virtue.

NATIVE SPIRIT

THE SUN DANCE WAY

Thomas Yellowtail

Recorded and edited by Michael Oren Fitzgerald

Introduction by Joe Medicine Crow

World Wisdom

Most recent printing indicated by last digit below
10   9   8   7   6   5   4   3   2

The publisher and the editor extend heartfelt thanks to the University of Oklahoma Press for allowing the use of excerpts of Thomas Yellowtail's words from his autobiography. Text from *Yellowtail: Crow Medicine Man and Sun Dance Chief*, by Michael O. Fitzgerald. Copyright © 1991 by the University of Oklahoma Press. Reprinted by permission of the publisher.

Cover photo: Crow Sun Dance, 1979
Frontispiece: Thomas and Susie Yellowtail, c. 1950

Book and cover design by Susana Marín

Library of Congress Cataloging-in-Publication Data
Yellowtail, Thomas.
Native spirit : the Sun Dance way / Thomas Yellowtail ; recorded and edited by Michael Oren Fitzgerald ; introduction by Joe Medicine Crow.
p. cm. -- (Treasures of the world's religions series)
Includes bibliographical references.
ISBN-13: 978-1-933316-27-7 (pbk. : alk. paper)
ISBN-10: 1-933316-27-6 (pbk. : alk. paper) 1. Sun dance--History. 2. Indians of North America--Religion. 3. Indian cosmology--North America. 4. Indians of North America--Rites and ceremonies. 5. Vision quests--North America. 6. Spiritual formation. I. Fitzgerald, Michael Oren, 1949- II. Title.

E98.D2Y45 2007
299.7'138--dc22
2006029319

All royalties from the sale of this book will be used to donate copies of the companion DVD to American Indian tribal colleges and high schools on reservations in the US and Canada

Printed on acid-free paper in China.
For information address World Wisdom, Inc.
P.O. Box 2682, Bloomington, Indiana 47402-2682
www.worldwisdom.com

CONTENTS

Thomas Yellowtail praying beside an uncovered Sweat Lodge

PREFACE

This is the remarkable story of the preservation of an ancient Plains Indian cultural and spiritual way of life in the face of a government bent on destroying American Indian traditions. The main focus of the book concerns the Crow-Shoshone Sun Dance, as told through the words of the most revered spiritual leader of the Crow tribe during the twentieth century, Thomas Yellowtail. The last part of this book contains the words of six different elders from six different tribes, demonstrating that this story is not unique to the Crow but is much the same for all American Indian people—a triumph of the Native Spirit.[1]

The Introduction by the ninety-two year old Crow tribal historian, Joe Medicine Crow,[2] poignantly tells the story of the Crow tribe's struggle to preserve their ancestral traditions during the first generations of reservation life when the U.S. government created policies designed to destroy Native lifeways, a struggle that is a common theme with all tribes. Medicine Crow explains how his tribe ultimately lost the form of their original Crow Sun Dance as a result of the government intervention and then adopted the Shoshone Sun Dance. He describes how John Trehero, a Shoshone Sun Dance chief, preserved the Shoshone Sun Dance, brought the Sun Dance to the Crow tribe, and eventually selected Thomas Yellowtail to be his successor as Sun Dance chief. Finally, he reveals insights into the current resurgence of interest in Native traditions and provides excellent advice that is addressed to American Indian youth, but which also applies to everyone seeking to find a balance in their lives.

The main part of this book is told in the words of Thomas Yellowtail.[3] The first and largest section of Yellowtail's narrative introduces the Crow-Shoshone Sun Dance, which is their most important sacred rite. There are also sections about the "Sweat Lodge," "The Vision Quest," and "Daily Prayer with the Pipe," the other three main rites of the Sun Dance Way. The final section of Yellowtail's words, "Advice for American Indian Youth," sets forth his essential philosophy, which applies equally to both Native and non-Native people.

American Indians are understandably reluctant to speak about their sacred ways to outsiders. However, over the last 150 years, spiritual leaders from many tribes

---

[1] When considering American Indian spirituality, it is evident that the many variations among the tribes are too vast to create a definitive statement that summarizes American Indian spirituality; but few would deny that there are unifying themes, including the sacred quality of virgin Nature, the need for purification in some form of Sweat Lodge ceremony and, above all, the idea of a Supreme Being. Among tribes of the high plains there are other unifying themes, including the Sun Dance, the Vision Quest, and the use of the Sacred Pipe in prayer. Although the form of the Sun Dance varies amongst the tribes of the high plains, the intention of personal, tribal, and world renewal through days of suffering and prayer is present in some degree.

[2] Dr. Joe Medicine Crow is also the oldest living Crow man and the last traditional "chief" of the Crow Nation. In pre-reservation days the title of "chief" was only awarded upon the successful completion of four different war deeds: leading a successful war party, stealing enemy horses, taking an enemy's weapon in battle, and counting first "coup" on an enemy. In World War II Joe Medicine Crow achieved all four of those war deeds, thus becoming the last traditional chief of the Crow tribe.

[3] In his later years Thomas Yellowtail felt compelled to preserve the sacred wisdom of his people for future generations, resulting in his autobiography entitled, *Yellowtail: Crow Medicine Man and Sun Dance Chief*, first published by the University of Oklahoma Press in 1991. The University of Oklahoma Press has graciously allowed the use of excerpts that constitute approximately six percent of Yellowtail's autobiography. Readers interested in additional information should consult the complete autobiography.

have spoken about their sacred ceremonies because they believed it was important to preserve their sacred wisdom for future generations. In most instances, their decisions were preceded by prayer and a request for guidance from their Medicine Fathers. Yellowtail's autobiography about the Crow-Shoshone Sun Dance is one example; this book and a companion documentary film of the same name were also approved by Thomas Yellowtail in 1992, one year before his death at age ninety.[4]

The documentary film, *Native Spirit*, contains the only known film footage ever taken of a Crow-Shoshone Sun Dance, which was held in honor of Thomas Yellowtail in 1989 at Wyola, Montana. Yellowtail not only asked me to film the Sun Dance, he directed where and when I filmed many parts of the four day rite.[5] He also approved all of the photographs I took during his life at more than a dozen Crow-Shoshone Sun Dances. In 1992 and 1993 I filmed interviews of Yellowtail speaking about the Crow Sun Dance, but we were unable to complete all of the interviews necessary for the documentary film prior to his death. The main narrative for *Native Spirit*, both the book and the primary documentary film, is therefore described in Yellowtail's own words taken from his memoirs. The film is presented in a double DVD set with numerous Special Features that include several of Yellowtail's film interviews.[6]

This book contains photographs from more than twenty Crow and Shoshone Sun Dances over the course of more than a century, from 1903 to 2004. Several of the photographs of the Crow Sun Dances in the 1940s have previously been published, but almost all of the remaining photographs have never been published before. I took the majority of the photographs used in the book at more than fifteen Sun Dances from 1971 through 2004; 26 photographs were taken by Åke Hultkrantz, the distinguished Swedish anthropologist who photographed several Shoshone Sun Dances in the 1940s, and the remaining Sun Dance photographs are from diverse sources.[7] The aggregation of these unpublished photographs from many sources results in the most comprehensive photographic book ever produced about the history of any Plains Indian Sun Dance.[8] The photographs of early reservation life

[4] Yellowtail's permission to produce and sell the film and books about the Sun Dance was on condition that neither he nor I would make any profit, so all royalties from every project involving Thomas Yellowtail are donated to benefit American Indians. All royalties from this book and the companion film will be used to donate copies of the film to American Indian tribal colleges and high schools on reservations in both the U.S. and Canada. All royalties from the sale of Yellowtail's autobiography are used to help support Crow and Shoshone Sun Dances and all royalties from *Indian Spirit*, for which he wrote the Introduction, are given to the Smithsonian's new Museum of the American Indian in Washington, D.C.

[5] I began taking most of the film from discrete places outside the Lodge, but Yellowtail repeatedly encouraged me to be bolder. Then he actually took me by the arm, brought me into the center of the Lodge and sat me down on a chair next to him in front of the dancers. The result is unhindered film of the sun dancers.

[6] Yellowtail hoped the film would be used in high school and college classrooms. Several of the Special Features are designed for classroom use and a teacher's guide is presented on the publisher's Internet site to facilitate the use of the DVD set in both high schools and colleges.

[7] The 1903 photograph was taken by William Wildschut, an ethnologist and photographer who worked on the Crow and Shoshone Reservations in the early part of the twentieth century. Wildschut was allowed extraordinary access to the Shoshone Sun Dance, which was held in violation of the government prohibitions against all traditional ceremonies. Diverse and unidentified photographers took the photographs of the Crow Sun Dances in the 1940s, '50s and '60s. Dennis Sanders, John Frost, and my wife, Judith, each took a handful of Sun Dance photographs from the 1970s and '80s.

[8] We were not able to reproduce any of the film of the Crow Sun Dance in the higher resolution necessary for this book; and the DVD contains more than one hundred photographs that could not be included in print due to space limitations. The DVD set is therefore the most comprehensive record of the Crow and Shoshone Sun Dance.

were taken by many photographers, mostly unknown, and are from diverse sources. I took all of the photographs of contemporary powwows and parades used in the book.

Between 2004 and 2006 I filmed interviews with seven elders representing seven different tribes: the Crow, Shoshone, Arapaho, Lakota, Cree, Salish, and Mescalero Apache.[9] These five men and two women are some of the most prominent American Indian leaders in North America, as revealed by their biographies on pages 99 to 101. Two film interviews with Joe Medicine Crow are combined into his Introduction; excerpts from interviews with the other six elders are transcribed and presented in the last section entitled "Conversations with Native Elders." Their comments are separated into three different sections, "Government Oppression and Cultural Preservation," "Tribal and Spiritual Life," and "Advice for Living in Two Worlds." These insights form an excellent complement to Yellowtail's words and Medicine Crow's Introduction because they demonstrate that the struggle endured by the Crow tribe is not unique, and that the miracle of cultural preservation and of a resurgence of interest in American Indian traditional lifeways is a living reality. The last section of "Advice for Living in Two Worlds" is addressed to Native youth, but their comments apply not only to American Indians but also to every person who is struggling to find a balance in his or her daily life in our fast-paced technological world.[10]

I join Thomas Yellowtail in his prayer that this book and the companion film are able to convey a small taste of the spiritual nature of the Sun Dance Way and that future generations will gain a better understanding of the depth and beauty of American Indian traditions.

Michael Fitzgerald
Bloomington, Indiana
June 2006

Michael Fitzgerald, Thomas
Yellowtail, and Susie Yellowtail
at Wyola, Montana, 1971

[9] Their film interviews are mixed into the body of the film and presented in Special Features on the DVD set.

[10] It is World Wisdom's intention to make extended film interviews available in video Slide Shows on www.worldwisdom.com. These Slide Shows will include subsequent film interviews with other spiritual leaders of different tribes and religions.

Crow camp, c. 1900

Medicine Crow, grandfather of Joe Medi-cine Crow

Hawk with the Yellow Tail Feathers and Lizzie Shane Yellowtail, parents of Thomas Yellowtail, and grandparents of Joe Medicine Crow

INTRODUCTION

I am ninety-two years of age now and I was brought up by my grandparents, Yellowtail and his wife Lizzie Yellowtail. Together they raised three sons, two daughters, and many grandchildren in their home just south of Lodge Grass, Montana. The Lodge Grass Valley is called the "Valley of the Chiefs" because of the many great war-chiefs who lived there in the early reservation years.

At the time when I was born in 1913 it was only about thirty years after the Crows were moved to this part of the reservation—reservation life actually started in 1884. My grandparents were pre-reservation Indians who lived before the reservation was set up. They would go camping, hunting, and the men went on the war path. They were always on the move; they were nomads who enjoyed the free life in a beautiful country.

In 1884, the Secretary of Interior issued the so-called "Secretary's Order" to 'detribalize' the Indian people and make them into white men as soon as possible—a unilateral cultural assimilation process. One of the first things they wanted to do was establish a school, a boarding school. The boarding school was set up about 1890 at Crow Agency with a boy's dormitory, girl's dormitory, the dining room, classrooms, and other facilities. The Crow children were required to be taken to that boarding school and left there, including very young kids, five, six, seven years old.

The Indian agent would send out his Indian policemen to collect the children—he had a force of Indian policemen. They were ruthless because they had to try to please the agent and, of course, they got paid, so they were his men, his Gestapo. Every once in a while they would go out throughout the country and look for kids age five and take them away from their parents and bring them to the boarding school. And there they would become like slaves; they were mistreated and some were even killed there. The girls had to cook, bake, and do the personal laundry for all of the B.I.A. employees in the area, not just the people at the school. The boarding school was a mean place. The children were forbidden to speak their Native language; if they would speak in the Crow language they had to chew a strong soap—it had a terrible taste. The kids also couldn't play any Indian games—they were forbidden to follow anything to do with the Native cultural ways. If they violated any of these rules they were not allowed to visit with their parents on the weekends or to go home for family visits. The school cut off their long hair—they gave the boys a complete "G.I." hair cut and threw away their braids. The girls had their hair bobbed short.

A lot of children died mysteriously. My grandfather, Chief Medicine Crow, raised a little Nez Perce baby boy. Chief Joseph and the Nez Perce camped near here on the Crow Reservation when the army was after them. In the night time the Crow would take food into the Nez Perce camp. Quite a few Nez Perce left their babies with the Crow.

Chief Joseph

Nez Perce child

The parents said, "When this thing is over, if we survive we will come back for them." But many of the Nez Perce parents never returned. So Chief Medicine Crow raised the Nez Perce baby as part of his family. The boy later had to go to the government boarding school. He was mistreated and he died there. No one knows exactly what happened. I think he was punished so hard that he died; this same thing happened to many other children.

When Bob Yellowtail was just five years old, his little old grandmother, her name was Bear Stays by the Side of the Water, took her grandson, her little tipi, and her horses and went to the Wolf Mountains where they hid all summer. But the police found out about it—probably somebody told them. When they found out that he and his grandma were out in the Wolf Mountains they went out there, looked for them, and found them. His dad, Yellowtail, followed the police so when they found Yellowtail's mother and his son he rode up and was right there with them. When they took the little boy away from his grandmother they were rough, putting the little boy over the back of the saddle to travel the thirty-five miles back to Crow Agency. So his father said, "Look he's just a baby. I'll take him to the boarding school tomorrow." The Indian police de-

Above: Indian students gardening; *Below*: Crow boarding school at Pryor, Montana

Chief Medicine Crow (1848-1922) with wife Medicine Mountain Sheep (1855-1947), grandparents of Joe Medicine Crow

Willow Creek Boarding School mess hall, 1907

Tom Torlino, Navajo from Arizona, on arrival at the Indian Training School, Carlisle, Pennsylvania

cided to let the father bring him in, so the next morning they took the little boy to the boarding school at Crow Agency and left him there. Many families can tell similar stories.

Over time, however, the parochial schools moved in. The first one was set up by the Catholics over at St. Xavier. Then in 1904 the Baptist people were asked to come and start a church and school. President Grant asked the denominations to help assimilate the Indians and the churches actively tried to convert the Indians away from their traditional ceremonials. Then almost every Christian denomination opened churches and schools on the reservation. The church schools taught the kids how to read and write; at the government schools the education didn't go past the sixth grade—they just stopped there and repeated the sixth grade, so even when they finished government boarding school the children could barely read and write. And, at the church schools they didn't mistreat the children like they did at the government boarding schools. So families sent their children to the church schools instead of the government boarding school. By about 1922 the government boarding school at Crow Agency closed because all of the children were sent by their families to the church schools. The government thought that if the Indians became Christians then they would turn away from their Crow traditions, and,

Baking bread at the Willow Creek Boarding School, c. 1907

of course, some Indians did turn away from the traditions; but most Indians embraced Christianity without abandoning their own cultural traditions. There was no problem in the Indian way; everyone had a little different way to pray—we had our own way—but everyone was praying to the same, one God. A man can be a good Catholic and a good Sun Dance man. Tom Yellowtail went to Reverend Petzolt's Baptist Boarding School, which was close to Lodge Grass. Tom was a good Baptist, but the next week he was a sun dancer—there was no problem.

The "Secretary's Order" of 1884 also prohibited the Indians from practicing all activities related to their culture, including singing, dancing, and all traditional ceremonials. The reservation police had the power to enforce this Order to prevent any traditional singing and dancing. The Crow people were afraid to even put on their Native costumes; they were told to wear overalls, white man's outfits—told to start becoming white men. Our people were forced to become farmers and give up their traditions. For fifty years there was a strict period of cultural transition. However, the government could not take away the intangible things; the Crow people still had their values, their traditional religion, and their philosophy—they kept them. During this time they had to go hide and perform some of their rituals—many

Tom Torlino after transformation at Carlisle, 1885

Laundry at the Crow Boarding School, Pryor, Montana

Waiting for rations, c. 1905

Crow Police, c. 1905-1911

families tried to keep their spiritual traditions alive in the secrecy of their homes. And, all of the clan rules were kept intact, right up to this day, which is a good thing because those are important rules to follow. So we survived with our values and most of our ceremonials—the tribal culture was kept alive.

In 1934 the Commissioner of Indian Affairs removed the prohibitions in connection with a so-called "Indian Re-organization Act," so from that time on the people could do their ceremonials. On the Shoshone Reservation they were Sun Dancing right away—I think they were hiding it and doing it all along. The Crow also started to resume many of our traditional ceremonials, but during the fifty year break when the Sun Dance was outlawed, the Crow lost their own form of the Sun Dance. In the 1930s some Crow men went to the Sun Dance on the Shoshone Reservation in Fort Washakie, where John Trehero was the Sun Dance chief. William Big Day was one of the Crow men who danced with Trehero down on the Shoshone Reservation. Then in 1941 William Big Day invited John Trehero to come to Pryor and lead a Shoshone Sun Dance on the Crow Reservation. That Sun Dance was a big success and was attended by Bob Yellowtail, the superintendent of the Crow Reservation.

John Trehero, 1972

The next summer was after the start of World War II and Bob Yellowtail was instrumental in asking John Trehero to come and lead a Sun Dance at Crow Agency for the service men. Because he was the tribal superintendent Yellowtail had workmen help put up a big Lodge. He contacted the various military installations where the Crow boys were stationed and asked for them to have a short vacation; many soldiers came to take part in the Sun Dance here at Crow Agency in 1942. I recall there were more than one hundred dancers. That Sun Dance was also a great success so the result was that the Crow have used the Shoshone Sun Dance ever since that time. After that John Trehero came every summer to lead a Sun Dance somewhere on the Crow Reservation. At first just the men danced, following the practice of the Shoshone tribe. Then one woman came into the Sun Dance Lodge and just fasted—she didn't dance. Later on more Crow women came into the Lodge to fast. Finally the women started to dance just like the men. The Crows added women sun dancers, that is the main difference between the Crow and the Shoshone Sun Dance because only men dance in the Shoshone Sun Dance.

Tom Yellowtail considered John Trehero as a relative and, of course, John considered Tom in the same way. When old John came over to the Crow Reservation he would stay with us here—we used to live just half a mile up from Yellowtail's house. Tom Yellowtail started sun dancing himself shortly after the big Sun Dance here—probably in about 1943. After he became a sun dancer he participated every year, sometimes here and sometimes he went to the Sun Dance with John at the Wind River Reservation. He was a very sincere sun dancer.

In about 1963 Trehero announced that he was going to retire, that his next Sun Dance would probably be his last one. He also an-

Crow sun dancers, 1941

Building a Crow Sun Dance
Lodge, 1940s

nounced that he was going to give his Sun Dance position to an eligible young man to carry on. Up to that point the Shoshone men as well as Crow sun dancers were always approaching John and asking him if he would give them his Sun Dance position; many men asked for that honor. But John always said, "I'll let you know when the time comes that my Medicine Fathers, the sacred protectors (I think they're the 'little people'), will tell me when and to whom to give the position." So, he announced that the time had come and that he was going to retire and turn the position of Sun Dance chief over to a good man who would take over and do a good job. Oh, all the dancers were quiet. Then John pointed at Tom Yellowtail and said, "I'm going to turn it over to him." It disappointed a lot of other men who wanted to be the Sun Dance chief.

Then the next year they had a Sun Dance up here on the Crow Reservation. That was when John officially turned the position over to Tom. Trehero himself didn't go into the dance but he kept telling Tom just what to do, when to do things, and so forth—he coached Tom along during that Sun Dance and, of course, he gave Tom all of the sacred Sun Dance objects, the medicine-fans and so forth. From that time forward Tom Yellowtail was the most important Sun Dance chief of the Crow tribe until his death in 1993 when he was ninety years of age.

The Shoshone people and the Crow people who have decided to become Sun Dance men would do so with a feeling and conviction that, after a time, they would acquire quite some power, the power to help people, the power to heal afflictions of the body, and to solve other problems. To me John Trehero, of all the Sun Dance men in Indian country, was the top man—the most powerful, the most authentic. I received a direct benefit of that power. In 1942 I was ready to leave for the war. Two days before I left I was given a little eagle plume that was dyed yellow that Trehero blessed and made into a medicine feather. So long as that little yellow eagle feather was in my helmet I was cool and collected and I knew just what to do. It kind of guided me on a safe road. Trehero's sacred medicine brought me safely through World War II; it allowed me to achieve success in my war deeds—that is my connection with John's power, I felt it. His sacred medicine also allowed many other Crow soldiers to achieve great war deeds.

And John gave his power to Tom Yellowtail. Tom himself would fast on Vision Quests and, of course, he was also fasting when he was in the Sun Dance. In that way Tom also acquired a lot of power; he helped a lot of sick people around here. Tom Yellowtail did a great deal to help the Crow tribe and perpetuate the Crow Sun Dance religion. The book about Tom Yellowtail's life and the Crow Sun Dance is also important because it preserves the wisdom of the old-timers for future generations. Tom Yellowtail is a great man.

John Trehero, 1940s

Thomas Yellowtail, 1972

Thomas Yellowtail in Switzerland, 1953

In about 1984 Tom Yellowtail chose a successor to carry on the Sun Dance and then just last year that position of Sun Dance chief was passed to a younger man to carry on. They had a powerful Sun Dance last summer; a lot of people were blessed. It is getting so that there are several Sun Dances each summer—all over the reservation many different men are holding Sun Dances. I don't know exactly where all of the men get their authority—probably from different medicine bundles—but there is a resurgence in the Sun Dance and this is a good thing. The Sun Dance legacy of John Trehero and Tom Yellowtail is being carried on.

My grandparents raised me more like a boy way back in 1840s and 1850s. They kept that up, notwithstanding the fact that I had to go to boarding school and learn the white man's language. They taught me to be an old traditional Crow Indian—my grandfather even made little bows and arrows for me. My youth was shaped by these old-timers who had lived the traditional nomadic life. Tom Yellowtail was my youngest uncle; he was about ten years older than me, so I also owe a lot of my childhood training to my Uncle Tom. Tom Yellowtail was a great athlete and taught me about farming, hunting, and trapping. He went on to help re-establish several forms of traditional dancing on the Crow Reservation, including the Tail Feather Society.

Tom Yellowtail and some other young men helped revive traditional dancing at the Crow Fair in the 1940s. Then in 1952 or '53 we started the All-American Indian Days in Sheridan, WY. Sheridan is close to the Crow Reservation so the Crow tribe was instrumental in hosting and putting on this celebration. This was the largest powwow in the United States for more than twenty years and attracted Indian people from all over the country. As part of the powwow we had a pageant to honor a Miss Indian America, who traveled during the year to teach young Indian school children about traditional values. I was one of the main program arrangers and an announcer. Each night we asked different tribes to present some representation of their tribal culture. Up to that time many of the tribes had stopped dancing and singing, so the All-American Indian Days was instrumental in bringing back the powwow.

Then over the years other tribes followed the example of the All-American Indian Days and started their own powwows. First the Arapaho held their own powwow in Ethete, then the Piegans held one each summer in Browning. Then attendance at the All-American Indian Days started dwindling because there was a powwow somewhere in Indian country almost every week during the summer, which was a good thing. When the powwow dancing came back there was a need for traditional costumes, so they revived the old handicrafts—the bead work, the quill work, that was almost forgotten. Some years ago they stopped having this powwow in Sheridan, but it established the way that other tribes hold their powwows and pageants to honor their youth and teach them about their traditions.

The powwow is a vehicle that is keeping our children "Indian." A lot of our Crow young people have long hair and they braid their hair nicely—not only the Crow but other tribes also. Of course they go to school, but during the Crow Fair you'll see even the little kids all dressed up, dancing, parading on horses, going back to the old Indian ways and enjoying themselves. They learn about clan rules, they meet their clan relatives, they learn about their traditions. Then they put their Indian costumes away and they go to school. I'm glad to see that they are hanging on to the old ways. So there is a sort of renaissance of going back to the Indian traditional ways all over the country. The powwow is turning the Indian back to the blanket—which is a good thing.

I have lived in two worlds: one is a traditional Crow Indian way—I dance, sing, and go to ceremonies and all those things; and at the same time, I have lived like a modern American, going to several colleges, and I had good jobs. I can mix the two, blend the two, get

Parade at Crow Fair

Powwow at Crow Fair

the best from each, and enjoy life living in both worlds. When I want to give advice to these young Crow Indian boys and girls, I tell them "never forget the old tribal ways, this brings a good life—use them." And I also tell them, "go to school, get a good education, and be able to compete in the white man's world in finding jobs, following your profession. You can blend the two and enjoy a good bi-cultural way." It is possible to live in both worlds. That is my advice to these young kids, and they are doing it now.

This project is going to help a lot of people, so I want to do my part with a Crow Indian prayer:

> Great Spirit, today it is my pleasure to have talked about the life of Tom Yellowtail, particularly about his work in the Sun Dance Way. It is important to carry on Tom Yellowtail's legacy of helping people through the Sun Dance Way, so I pray for Mike and his son here, these friends of ours from Indiana, that they may go home, get home safely, and complete their work. *Aho! Aho!*

Joe Medicine Crow
Lodge Grass, MT
March, 2005

Opposite: Yellowtail praying beside an uncovered Sweat Lodge at his home near Wyola, Montana, 1980s
Above: Crow Sun Dance, 1970s

Opening Prayer

Acbadadea, *Maker of All Things Above, hear my prayer. Now we have filled our pipe and offered our smoke to the Heavens Above, to Mother Earth, and to the directions of the Four Winds. Before we start our work, we must send this prayer. Medicine Fathers from all the four directions of the world, hear my prayer. Acbadadea, I send this prayer to You as I am going to speak about our sacred ways.*

Acbadadea *is the Creator, the Maker of All Things Above, Who is above and beyond this world but Who has created and continues to give life to this world. When we pray, we always say, "Acbadadea, Maker and Creator of All Things, we pray to you."*

Thomas Yellowtail saying a prayer during the morning Sunrise Ceremony of a Sun Dance, 1979

Sun Dance Lodge complete before the start of the rite

THE SUN DANCE

When we speak about the Sun Dance Religion we include the Sweat Lodge, the Vision Quest, and daily prayer with the Indian Pipe. But the Sun Dance Ceremony contains our entire religion, and it is our most important rite.

Above: Crow sun dancers in the 1980s
Below: Crow Sun Dance in 1940s

When the Sun Dance comes up, some people go in and participate, and when it is over, they don't show up at monthly prayer meetings or pray during the year at all. I don't call that a sincere member. They should remember the Sun Dance way of prayer ... to take a smoke and say prayers by themselves, wherever they are, every day, if they want to consider themselves members of the Sun Dance Religion.

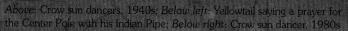

Above: Crow sun dancers, 1940s; *Below left:* Yellowtail saying a prayer for the Center Pole with his Indian Pipe; *Below right:* Crow sun dancer, 1980s

The Center Pole is always a cottonwood tree. On the day before the lodge is to be erected, we go to bring in the Center Pole. It's heavy; quite a lot of men will go. We come to it and we have a ceremony before we cut the Center Pole.

I smoke my Indian pipe and offer a prayer…
"Now we're going to use you; at our Sun Dance we are going to use you. You are going to be the center tree. On you will be the bird; the eagle will be there and the buffalo will be up there, placed on you. You will be the staff of this dance that is coming up; it is you who will join us to all of the Powers of the universe, to Acbadadea. People will come to you; markings will be put on you indicating the number of days that we will spend with you. The power will be placed on you. The Medicine Fathers will be there on the center tree, and the sun dancers will put their hands on you and say their prayers, and we want you to help us. We want you to have moisture that you will provide us, for we are not drinking, we are not eating, we'll be suffering. We'll come to you and put our hands on you and give prayers to all of the Medicine Fathers who are going to be on you, watching all of the dancers to see who is sincere. When the sun dancers are through with their smoke and prayer, they will put the ashes of their smoke at your base on the ground where you are to be set up. That is for you. Through you we will send our prayers, and from you, we will receive all of the blessings from above. Help us."

Above: Cutting the Center Pole, Shoshone Sun Dance, 2004
Below: Eagle and buffalo in Crow Sun Dance Lodge, 1970s

Above: Singing the Tree Song, Crow Sun Dance, 1981
Below: Singing the Tree Song, Shoshone Sun Dance, 1940s

Before raising the Center Pole we sing the Tree Song. The Center Pole is lying on the ground. We sing the song, repeating it four times, and then we whoop and holler and reach down and grasp the tree and lift it about four feet off the ground. Then we put it down. We repeat the sacred song four times, and we lift the tree up four times and lay it down again, four times.

There are long ropes running around the fork of the tree so the men can keep the tree from swaying. Some large poles about twenty feet long are used to help raise and guide it, as up, and up, the tree goes, until the butt of the tree drops into the hole that has been dug for it. Now it stands there. We put dirt around the base and tamp it in tight so that the pole is straight and the opening of the fork faces East.

Raising the Center Pole, Crow Sun Dance, 1981

The outside ring of the Sun Dance Lodge is made by the upright cotton-wood trees. Each of the twelve pine rafter poles that meet at the Center Pole is placed into one of the upright cotton-wood forks. This makes the sacred circle of the Lodge. The rafter poles link the sacred circle to the Center Pole, which is the sacred point where all three worlds are connected…the physical world of the tribe…the spiritual world of our Medicine Fathers…and the pure world of Acbadadea.

The Lodge is ready before the start of the Crow Sun Dance, 1970s

The Lodge is round, and that represents the earth, which is round. The twelve poles, leading from each forked pole to the center, represent the circle of the twelve months of the year. Each of the twelve poles represents a month of the year when we must have our monthly Sun Dance prayer meeting.

Above: Building the Lodge, Crow Sun Dance, Pryor, Montana, 1941
Below: Crow Sun Dance Lodge, 1950s

People of the tribe who are not dancing will set up their camps in a large circle around the place where the Sun Dance Lodge is to be constructed. No tents are set up to the East. It makes a sacred circle of everyone who comes to share prayers at the Sun Dance.

Above: Crow Sun Dance camp, 1981
Below: Shoshone Sun Dance camp, 2004

There is the outside circle of all the tribal camps that surrounds the inner circle of the Sun Dance Lodge. Prayers flow from the tribal circle to the Sun Dance Lodge, and blessings flow from the Center Pole of the Lodge to the tribal circle, and then to all of the created world. Everyone in the camp circle can feel the power that is being generated through the Sun Dance Lodge. For several days, the Sun Dance is the center of the reservation and many spectators will camp and attend to show their support for the dancers. Even if people have not fulfilled their religious duties during the rest of the year, the Sun Dance brings everyone together in prayer for three days each summer.

Above: Shoshone Sun Dance, 1940s
Below: Crow Sun Dance, 1972

The clothing that the dancers wear
expresses their humility as they prepare to stand at the center of the universe. Each man will wear, wrapped
around his waist, a skirt that goes
to his ankles. A belt or sash of some
kind will hold the skirt. The men
will be bare-chested.

Crow sun dancers, 1970s

The women will have on simple cotton dresses that they have made. But all of the dancers, men and women alike, usually wrap themselves in a blanket as they march into the Lodge. All dancers will be barefooted, for no one may wear shoes inside the sacred circle.

Crow sun dancers, 1970s

Every dancer will have an eagle bone whistle hanging around his neck. The whistles are made from the longest bone in an eagle's wing, and each whistle has an eagle plume attached to the end which flies as the whistle is blown. Each dancer also holds an eagle plume in each hand.

Above and Below left: Crow Sunrise Ceremony, 1979
Below right: Eagle bone whistle, 1940s

The buffalo will face the sponsor and the Sun Dance chief during the dance. We place a bundle of sweet sage in each nostril of the buffalo to represent the buffalo's breath offering a prayer to Acbadadea. In the same manner a sincere person's breath can carry a prayer.

Crow Sun Dance Lodges, 1970s

When we blow our eagle bone whistles during the Sun Dance, our breath does carry a continual prayer. While the singers are beating on the drum and singing, the dancers are blowing on the eagle bone whistles. The drumming is the heartbeat of the universe. And the heartbeat, and the breath of the eagle bone whistles, send a prayer to all of the Medicine Powers in the universe, and to Acbadadea.

Shoshone sun dancers, 1940s

Just before dusk each dancer must be dressed in his Sun Dance clothes and proceed to the Lodge. All the dancers gather behind the Lodge, facing East. The Sun Dance chief and the sponsor each lead one line into the Lodge. After the solemn entry procession, the family members bring in the bedrolls for the dancers. Now they are going to be in this spot for three or four days … dancing, praying, and sleeping in this spot.

Above: Crow sun dancers lining up before entering the Lodge, 1980s; *Below left*: Shoshone sun dancers, 1940s
Below right: Thomas Yellowtail outside the Lodge after a Sunrise Ceremony, 1972

*Once we sing the four sacred Morning Songs, the singers will start
up the drum and we will dance late into that night.*

Shoshone singers, 1940s

Above: Crow sun dancers at night by the light of the sacred fire, 1970s
Below: Crow sun dancers, 1970s

The Morning Prayer and morning Sunrise Ceremony are two of the most important parts of the Sun Dance. All our different kinds of prayer during the day and during the year are important. But the prayer at the Sun Dance during the sunrise greeting is one of the most important.

The dancers are up before the sun rises. They wake each other up, and the announcer will call ... "Get up, all you dancers. The sun will soon rise and we've got to have the ceremony, dancing to the rising sun."

Above: Crow Sunrise Ceremony, 1980s
Right: Susie Yellowtail, 1979

All the dancers, including the women, will gather in the center of the Lodge and line up facing the East towards the entrance of the Lodge. Now the singers start the sunrise song. They sing that song before the sun peeps over the hill, and they will sing maybe for five, ten minutes, while the dancers face the direction of the morning sun and blow on their eagle bone whistles.

Crow Sunrise Ceremonies, 1970s

The moment the first streak of light comes up over the hill, all the dancers stretch out their hands towards the sun, and then pass them over their body to bless themselves. After the whole sun has risen over the horizon, the song ends.

This is a very sacred time.

Sunrise over a Crow Sun Dance Lodge, 2004

After the sun is up and the song ends, the male dancers gather around the fire-place that has been burning all night. Plenty of hot coals are there. We sit by the sacred fire, in a horseshoe shape around it. We don't close the passageway to the East. The singers will pause. Everything is to be quiet, for we dancers have four songs to sing in order. All of them have to be sung four times over, followed by blowing the whistles four times.

Crow Sunrise Ceremonies, 1970s

In our morning Sunrise Ceremony, when we sing the four sacred songs after we have greeted the rising sun, we bring forward all of the Medicine Fathers, and all of the sacred beings in the universe hear our prayers.

Crow Sunrise Ceremony, 1973

After all the songs are completed, the sponsor or I will get up and put sweet cedar on the fire. We put the cedar onto the hot coals and the smoke rises and goes all over the lodge giving blessings.

In the Sun Dance Way, the individual benefits from his prayers, but also, the entire tribe benefits from the Sun Dance, because part of our prayers are especially for the tribe and for all creation.

Below: Crow Sun Dance camp, 1970s; *Above right*: Thomas Yellowtail praying after the sunrise, 1970s

When I say the Morning Prayer after we finish the songs, I ask that the tribe and the entire creation be blessed for another year until the next Sun Dance. All of the other dancers share in this prayer. This is a very important time and anyone who is present can sense that we are all at the heart of creation during these prayers.

After the Sunrise Ceremony, when the singers start beating on the drum, many of the dancers will arise and begin to dance. Each one will stand in his place and face the Center Pole. The Center Pole contains all of the sacred power of the universe and as the dancers concentrate on the center tree, so also do they concentrate their prayers on Acbadadea.

Above and Opposite: Shoshone sun dancers, 1940s

The dancers know the songs being sung and at a certain moment in the song, each dancer knows it is time to run toward the Center Pole. Many of the dancers will run in a straight line toward the pole, then stop and dance back towards their position in the circle of the Lodge, while always concentrating on the center tree. The dancer may fix his eyes on a certain spot on the tree, or on the buffalo, or the eagle. The dancer's gaze will remain fixed on that place for the entire time he, or she, is dancing.

We are not drinking any water nor eating anything for three or sometimes four days, and we are burning up. The hot summer sun burns, and your body is burning up because you are dry. Some tribes allow their dancers to drink after sundown during each day of the Sun Dance, but we don't. We allow no drinks or food for the entire duration of the Dance. So all the dancers just about torture themselves.

Below left: Shoshone sun dancers, 1940s; *Below right:* John Trehero, 1972

Above: Crow sun dancers, 1950s
Below: Shoshone sun dancers, 1940s

Above: Crow Sun Dance, 1941
Below: Shoshone Sun Dance, 1940s

Above: Crow Sun Dance, 1941
Below left: Crow Sun Dance, 1940s
Below right: Crow sun dancers, 1970s

Crow Sun Dance, 1979

On the second morning, the dancers again blow their whistles to the rising sun and sing the sacred morning songs. The dancers know on this morning that their most difficult day is before them, so, as they listen to the prayers of the Sun Dance chief, they pray to the Medicine Fathers to give them strength.

Above: John Trehero at Shoshone Sunrise Ceremony, 1940s; *Below:* Thomas Yellowtail at Crow Sunrise Ceremony, 1979

Crow Sunrise Ceremonies, 1979

In the same way that the buffalo is painted to make his medicine stronger, the dancers are painted on the second day to give them strength for their spiritual warfare. The warrior fights an enemy who is on the outside, while the sun dancer wages a war on an enemy within himself.

Just as the warriors of olden days put on their finest headdresses and feathers ... painted themselves, and made medicine in preparation for battle, so too do the sun dancers prepare for their most difficult sacred ordeal on the second day of the Sun Dance.

The dancers have all suffered the first day and their prayers have been heard by the Medicine Fathers. Now the power in the lodge and on the center tree is great, and all those present can feel the radiation of this spiritual presence.

Above: Crow Sun Dance, 1989; *Below:* Shoshone Sun Dance, 1940s

The dancers have changed their dress in honor of this spiritual presence. They are preparing to give up all of their remaining individual strength through more suffering in order to place themselves at the mercy of the Medicine Fathers. Now the sun dancers prepare for their spiritual warfare.

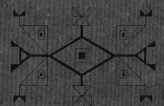

Above: Shoshone Sun Dance, 1940s
Below: John Trehero at Crow Sun Dance, 1973

As we begin our second day, we start to get dry and weak. Our friends, our folks on the outside who are not dancing, will go out to get little trees. They will cut small cottonwood trees, probably about two or three inches thick, and set them up for each individual dancer to make what we call "stalls." To make the stalls, one cottonwood is set up on each side of every dancer's place so that when the dancer is standing, waiting to advance toward the Center Pole, he can grasp them to keep from falling, for we are getting weak.

Above: Crow sun dancers, 1970s
Below right: Robert Yellowtail outside the Sun Dance Lodge, 1970s

All the people of the tribe can see how the dancers are suffering. They know the prayers of the dancers are made on behalf of the whole tribe. Sometimes an elder will stand by the singers and offer his own song ... a song to encourage the dancers, to tell them what they are doing is good and that the tribe appreciates their sacrifice. This gives the dancers strength to go on.

Above left: Crow singers at the drum, 1970s; *Above right*: Crow singers at the drum, 1970s; *Below*: Crow Sun Dance, 1941

Crow sun dancers, 1970s

Crow sun dancers, 1950s

Crow Sun Dance, 1970s

Throughout that day I will be doctoring, even until midnight.

When people come in to be healed, they are coming onto holy ground. They come in and stand before the center tree. I generally ask them their ailments and they tell me, and I pray accordingly, with my feather and medicines, to one or all of the Medicine Fathers.

Above and Opposite above: Thomas Yellowtail doctoring his grandson, 1979

"Help me, Medicine Fathers; you are right here on the tree. The tree has the power; the power is placed on that center tree, and it is great."

Before I work on a patient, I touch the center tree to get more power from my fathers that I'm going to work with. We will have the patient put their hands against the center tree and then get behind them and touch them from head to feet.

Left: Thomas Yellowtail dancing back to his stall after doctoring

Wherever their ailments are, I touch that spot and put the feathers there, and then I draw the sickness out of the patient and toss it to the East. I say: "Go on and on to the ocean where you'll drift away and not return to this person."

Above: John Trehero doctoring, Shoshone Sun Dance, 1940s
Below: Doctoring at Shoshone Sun Dance, 1940s

In doctoring a patient, some of my strength, of my own body, goes out. I use a consider-able amount of my own strength, giving some of it to the patient that I'm working on. Sometimes dancers come up to the Center Pole to be doctored, but mostly it is people from the tribe who come into the Lodge to receive its blessings and ask for my prayers with the Medicine Fathers to cure their ailments. So, after working on many people all day long, probably fifty people or more, I feel exhausted.

Thomas Yellowtail doctoring, Crow Sun Dance, 1970s

Family members, friends, and people from all over the reservation bring in cattails from the creeks and sweet sage and mint from the fields. They also bring tobacco as an offering to the dancers. The announcer calls the dancer to the Lodge entrance to receive his gift. When the dancer returns to his stall, he will place the cattails on the ground and make a bed of them to lie upon. The cattails are cool and they comfort the dancers. The sage and mint will be placed around the stall so that their scent will fill the entire Lodge. This gives great relief from the ordeal and these gifts are appreciated by all the dancers.

Crow sun dancers receive cattails, 1950s

Above: Crow sun dancers receive gifts, 1970s; *Below:* Crow sun dancers receive cattails, 1950s

The dancers will also receive tobacco with a prayer request. Later they will offer a prayer on behalf of the person who presented it. You can see how the support of the entire tribe flows into the Lodge and in turn how the prayers from the Sun Dance are returned to the tribe. It is a participation by the entire tribe in the sacred ceremony and because of this our tribe receives new strength with which to face the new year.

Opposite: Sun dancer praying with a sacred Pipe at the Center Pole, 1979
Above: Crow singers, 1950s; *Right*: Crow sun dancer outside the Lodge after the Sunrise Ceremony, 1970s

The most sincere dancers will dance almost continually for the three days, even though they have no food or water for this entire time. They will always be up, going forward to the center tree, and dancing back to their place, while always facing the tree and concentrating on their spot, day after day. These dancers will be given something by the Medicine Fathers, especially by the buffalo. Each dancer is beginning to get dry and to suffer, and those who keep going continually, even after they start suffering, will be rewarded by the buffalo. It generally does not happen early in the Dance, but on the second day.

Above: Shoshone Sun Dance, 1903; *Below:* John Trehero at Crow Sun Dance, 1973

Finally, the Medicine Fathers will take pity on a dancer and give him a vision. They are present on the center tree, and they see into the hearts of everyone. This is a great moment for the dancer who receives the vision and also for the entire tribe.

Above: Crow Sun Dance Lodge, 1970s
Below: Crow sun dancer, 1970s

When a dancer is to receive a vision, he takes a fall. He lies there, unconscious. When that happens, we hurriedly go and cover him up with cattails and sweet sage. Then we pray for him. He is gone into a vision, so nobody bothers him.

Crow Sun Dance, 1970s

The reward is medicine coming from the Sun Dance, given to him by the buffalo. The buffalo will give the dancer something … probably tell him what to do; what kind of feathers, colors, or medicine to make. Different persons will receive different things. After he has received his reward, he will wake up and he is ready to get up and dance again. A person should not be afraid when this thing happens.

Left: Shoshone Sun Dance, 1940s; *Below right*: Crow sun dancer, 1970s

The morning of the third day is a wonderful time, both because of the great blessing of the Sunrise Ceremony but also because of the blessings which are now greater than ever all over the Lodge and among the dancers.

Above right: Crow Sunrise Ceremony, 1980s; *Below*: Crow Sun Dance Lodge, 1950s

Around noon, or perhaps a little after, it is time to bring in the water to break the fast. The sponsor will select four women to go and bring it. Before it is served, the sponsor will call someone to come forward and bless the water. Then the water is passed to all of the dancers as they are seated in their stalls.

Above: Four women ready to distribute water, 1970s; *Below:* Shoshone sun dancers start to break their fast with sacred water, 1940s

Now the ordeal is over.

Above: Empty stalls, Shoshone Sun Dance, 1940s
Below: Crow Sun Dance Lodge, 1970s

Above: Clan relatives praying for Crow sun dancers after they have broken the fast but before they leave the Lodge, 1980s
Below: Shoshone Sun Dance Lodge after the ceremony has ended, 1940s

Leaving the Lodge, Crow, 1979

A person might never receive a great vision or any power — it doesn't matter. The Medicine Fathers know what is in our hearts, and they may help us or bless us in ways we do not see. We must be resigned to whatever trials they send us and we must be content with what we have been given. If a person expects to receive something great, then that person will probably never receive anything. The Medicine Fathers do not owe anything to anyone. We must realize this and dedicate our lives to living in accordance with the directions given to us from Above — not just once a year, but every day and year after year.

Above: Thomas Yellowtail, 1979; *Below:* Crow Sun Dance Lodge, 1980s
Opposite: Crow Sun Dance Lodge after the Sun Dance, 2000

Now I am speaking about the Sun Dance Religion and I have done my best to speak with my heart. There is much more that could be said about the Indian Way, but enough has been said so that each person who hears these words can know that the Sun Dance Religion is a path that can lead us through this life and lead us to Acbadadea.

K2519-07

DAILY PRAYER WITH THE PIPE

The presence of the Pipe, the preparation for its use, and the prayers that are offered through its smoke, hold a central position in the daily life of a traditional Indian.

The Pipe is the sacred form that was given to us for our prayers, but it is the smoke that offers the prayer. It is the tobacco that is changed to smoke, and the smoke that carries our prayers to the Four Winds and to Acbadadea. It is important to offer prayers correctly with smoke.

First, after you light the Pipe, you must offer it with the stem pointed upward to Acbadadea, the Maker of All Things Above. Then come down with the stem toward Mother Earth, and then to all the four directions of the wind. Of course you should also call upon all of your individual Medicine Fathers to be present. Then take a few puffs on the Pipe and say your prayers.

Some of our sacred rites, like the Sun Dance, recur once in the cycle of every year, but the prayer of the Pipe recurs in the cycle of each day, and this is a great thing. It is one of the main duties of every member of the Sun Dance Religion: to offer a prayer with a smoke at least twice a day, to pray every day through the offering of the smoke in the morning and in the evening, following the circle of the day from morning until night.

In the morning as I wake up, I say, "Aho! Father, thank you for letting me sleep through the night and see another day. This is a start of another day. Today, whatever we do, be with us and guide us, watch us and protect us. Let us live through this day, helping each other."

After we go through that day and nightfall comes, when it is time to go to bed, I will say a prayer again as I offer my smoke: "Father, this is the end of the day and time for us to sleep now. Thank you for watching over us and guiding us during this day. Watch us now and give us a good night's rest and good dreams so we may live as we should tomorrow."

As we smoke the Pipe and offer our prayer with each new day, we should remember the importance of having a sacred center within us and that this sacred presence is represented by the Pipe. It is the Pipe that connects us with Acbadadea. In these days the Pipe may have an even greater importance because some of our other rites of the olden-day Indians are gone.

While the prayer with the Pipe will start and end the day, it is also important to pray during the day. Each day, whatever I am doing, I am always praying and thinking of God. As I work along, whether I am out in the field, or wherever, I am always praying right along when I am alone. I say, that if you look for them, then you will find many parts of the day that could be spent in praying, remembering the name of God. For a Crow, repeating Acbadadea is probably the best short prayer during the day.

We should pray that people will see that the answer to their problems is to follow their religion and to pray. We should also realize that God may not answer all our prayers. God knows best and His ways are not always easy for us to understand. It may be that something you have prayed for will not come to pass. If this is so, it is because of a greater purpose that we cannot know, and we must resign ourselves to God's judgment. So when I pray with the Pipe, I always ask for the understanding of God's purpose so that I may follow His path.

THE SWEAT LODGE

We participate in the Sweat Lodge ceremony throughout the year to prepare ourselves for the Sun Dance, so it is an important part of the Sun Dance Religion. When a person has the proper intention and observes all of the rules, the Sweat Lodge purifies the person not only on the outside, but also throughout his inner being.

The Sweat Lodge is called the little brother of the big Lodge … the Sun Dance Lodge. It is similar in construction. You cut twelve small poles from tree saplings and bend them over and tie them together. You should say a prayer before cutting each tree, because the tree has allowed us to use it for our prayer ceremony. I have already spoken about the meaning of the form of the Sun Dance Lodge, and this meaning is also true for the Sweat Lodge.

Above: Thomas Yellowtail building a Sweat Lodge; *Below:* Crow Sweat Lodge without the cover

We should always offer a smoke and prayer before, and after, each Sweat Lodge ceremony. We will bring sweet grass, sweet cedar, or sweet sage into the Lodge and purify the whole Lodge with the smoke before we start. We can also purify the Lodge with the smoke from the kinnikinnik tobacco used in the Pipe while we pray.

When everyone is in the Sweat Lodge and the door is closed, we begin to say our prayers. As we pray we throw dippers of water on the rocks and steam fills the entire Lodge. The prayers are the same as the Sun Dance prayers we have talked about. All of the participants should be praying right along during the entire ceremony. Everyone may not be praying out loud; that doesn't matter. But one should pray in one's heart during a sacred ceremony; that is the purpose of the ceremony: to purify the participants both inside and outside.

Above left: Yellowtail's Sweat Lodge; *Above right*: Shoshone Sweat Lodge at Fort Washakie
Middle left: Preparing the rocks in the fire; *Middle right*: Red hot rocks
Below left: Tending the fire and the rocks; *Below right*: Taking the hot rocks into the Sweat Lodge

There is no light in the Lodge except the red glow of the hot rocks. The smell of the sacred incense fills the air. We have entered into another world which is beyond our physical world. When the water is thrown onto the rocks, the heat does not merely cleanse us on the outside; it also goes all the way into our hearts. We know that we must suffer the ordeal of the heat in order to purify ourselves. In that way, we can re-emerge from the Sweat Lodge at the end of the ceremony as new men who have been shown the light of the wisdom of our spiritual heritage for the first time. This allows us to participate in all of our daily tasks with the fresh remembrance of our position on earth and our continuous obligation to walk on this earth in accordance with the sacred ways.

Above: Closing the door of a Shoshone Sweat Lodge
Below: During a Shoshone Sweat Lodge ceremony

THE VISION QUEST

Before a man goes out on a Vision Quest, he must first consult with a medicine man. A man must be humble before the great mysteries will grant him anything. A humble man will ask for guidance from a spiritual man. The instructions for the prayer may depend on the young man's intention.

When people want to go fasting, they first prepare themselves by taking a sweat bath to purify themselves. It is very important to undergo a purification before and after every major undertaking. Right after he or she is through with the sweat bath, the vision seeker will go and spend three or four days upon the hill or high mountains.

In the olden days, the man going out to seek his vision would wear a buffalo robe, moccasins, and sometimes a loincloth. When he reached the area of the retreat, he removed all of his clothing and almost always was exposed to Nature unless he covered himself with his robe while he slept. I instruct those who ask my advice to follow the traditional way of the old timers

When a person is on a Vision Quest, he must have certain attitudes and intentions for his prayers to be sincere, and then he must carry these over into his daily life. If you participate because you know the purpose of the rites and you want to express your gratitude and love of the sacred ways, then you may eventually receive a great reward.

Above: Crow Heart Butte, WY, a favorite Vision Quest site of the pre-reservation Crow and Shoshone tribes.

For those who have been sincere in the solitary invocation, Acbadadea will send a reward in the form of some medicine power. There are many different medicines a person can receive in different ways: different animals, different birds, or one of the powers of the universe. When a person returns to the world after a Vision Quest, he must take a sweat bath using sage to purify himself again before he gets back among his people. Then the meaning of the vision must be explained by the medicine men at home. The medicine man knows what must be done by the recipient of the medicine in order for him to protect it. The recipient of the medicine usually is instructed to make a medicine bundle that will preserve and protect the medicine power. These bundles serve as a constant reminder of the spiritual gifts we have been given and the corresponding attitudes which must always be present in order to safeguard our spiritual blessings.

Above: Medicine bundle hanging on tripod behind the owner's tipi, Crow, 1950s
Below right: Medicine bundle hanging on a tripod

ADVICE FOR AMERICAN INDIAN YOUTH

Everyone can see how things have changed from the olden times, when sacred values were at the center of our life, up to the present day, when our society does not seem to have a sense of the sacred. If people continue on their present course, with no prayer and no respect for sacred things, then things will get worse and worse for everyone. So many young people wonder what may happen to this world that we are in, and what they should do if they want to follow a spiritual path. They may think, "Do I have an opportunity to lead a life in accordance with the traditional ways?"

It is important for the young people to understand and follow their traditional religion. Each man will pass from this earth in his own time. Some of the prophecies talk only about the end of time; others speak about the break-up of the modern world as we know it and a return to the traditional ways of our ancestors. I can't say what will happen and whether we will find the spiritual ways of our ancestors in this world or another; but I do know that in either case we still have to make a choice, each one of us must choose at this present moment which path to follow. Each person's prayers can help everyone. The person who prays and remembers God will receive the greatest benefit for himself and for others.

There is nothing more I can say except to raise my voice in prayer:

"All the people should unite and pray together, regardless of their beliefs. You have given different ways to different people all over the world. As we know, this earth is round like a wagon wheel. In a wagon wheel, all the spokes are set into the center. The circle of the wheel is round and all spokes come from the center and the center is You, Acbadadea, The Maker of All Things Above. Each spoke can be considered as a different religion of the world which has been given by You to different people and different races. All of the people of the world are on the rim of the wheel and they must follow one of the spokes to the center. The different paths have been given to us but they all lead to the same place. We all pray to the same God, to You. Help us to see this wisdom. Aho! Aho!"

Above left: Plenty Coups, Absaroke; *Above right*: Washakie, Shoshone
Below left: Pretty Shield, Absaroke; *Below right*: Medicine Mountain Sheep (Mrs. Medicine Crow), Absaroke

CONVERSATIONS
with NATIVE ELDERS

The following interviews are with seven of the most prominent American Indians in North America representing the Arapaho, Cree, Crow, Lakota, Mescalero Apache, Salish, and Shoshone people. The biographies of these five men and two women are presented on pages 99 to 101.

Government Oppression and Cultural Preservation

There are a lot of challenges that our people have faced and a lot of challenges our ancestors had to face throughout history, especially in the last 500 years. When you look at everything that was against them it is really a wonder that our people are still here today — the disease, the government policies. The United States Government actually put bounties on Indian people's heads. There were later governmental policies that tried to take our land from us and take away our traditional ways. In my grandmother's generation, the children were taken from their homes and if the parents did not send their kids to school they were arrested. The police would actually come out to the homes, take the kids from their homes, and bring them to the boarding school. In the boarding schools the children were not able to see the way traditional families lived; they weren't able to see the way that you interact with children, the way that you raise children, the way you teach them traditional values. I think the government intended to help the Indian people to become part of the melting pot of America, so they wanted to teach Indian children not to speak the language, not to take part in the ancestral ceremonies, to turn away from all of these things so that they could become a part of the rest of American society. It was really detrimental to our people because that's who they were and that's what they were; so by teaching them that those things weren't good the government was basically telling them that they were not good. It was really devastating to our people. I think that our children today need to realize that the traditional ways are good and come from the Creator and that we can be a part of American society but also hold onto our traditional values, still hold onto our traditional teachings.

James Trosper, Shoshone/Arapaho

—James Trosper
Shoshone/Arapaho

I know that it's very difficult for young people, American Indian people or indigenous people living today, to try to figure out, "Do I follow the path of my elders or do I follow the path that I am learning in school?" Or, "Which way should I go?" I understand that these questions can be very, very confusing because of what has happened to indigenous people historically, with not only federal government policy but also with the role of churches stripping us of our normal religious traditions and cultural traditions. We find ourselves now in a situation in America where we have people who are understanding what has happened because they've studied the history and they've looked at what "missionization" has done to us — by that I mean missionaries coming to our reservations or trying to find us and converting us away from our Indian ways into being more like mainstream society. That process always creates a problem because we have our own inner voice; a little voice inside of us is telling us "you're really Indian, so why are you going that way?" Yet there is so much pressure in American society not to follow our inner voice and therefore to abandon our Native traditions because we're also Americans. So it's been very, very difficult for not only the young people, but also middle-aged Native people and our elders to continue to hang onto those traditions.

—Inés Talamantez
Mescalero Apache

Theresa Trosper and Cornesa Carusona, Shoshone

Zedora Enos, Shoshone, granddaughter of John
Trehero and great granddaughter of Chief Washakie

Consider this: there are many of our elders who were raised by their grandparents — people in our communities, who are 65, 75, maybe 80, raised by their grandparents. Their grandparents were raised by their grandparents. In three or four generational skips, you can connect to the people in the Buffalo Days. You could know the war deeds of some of our most famous warriors. You could know the medicines of some of our lady medicine people, just by asking your grandmother, who was raised by her grandmother, who was raised by her grandmother. And sometimes you think, "Well, Grandma, you know it's a long way from the Buffalo Days or a long way from the days of our strongest traditions." But it isn't. And you, yourself, if you were raised by your grandparents, you have a window into a world of our most beautiful traditions, our most useful and strong traditions, each with strong spirituality. And you in turn, can know these things and hand them onto new generations.

—Janine Pease
Crow/Hidatsa

I lost my daughter and her husband, who had four kids. When I became the guardian of my grandchildren I moved from Los Angeles back here to Saskatchewan to raise them on the Poundmaker Reserve — the Poundmaker First Nation. We have the Sweat Lodge right here; we don't have one in L.A. We have our Sun Dances, we have other sacred ceremonies, we have our drum here, we have our songs, and we have our Pipe here. I choose to live here with my relatives, the rest of the Cree, because I feel that my grandchildren need to know who they are. They need to retain their value system, they need to know and retain our belief systems, our world view as Cree, First Nations people here in North America.

—Gordon Tootoosis
Cree

Arvol Looking Horse and a young friend in Culver, Indiana

It wasn't professors or teachers that helped me get to the place where I am now; it was my elders. It was my father, a man who went to the third grade but understood our traditions; it was my uncles and my aunts. And, yes, in some ways it was also my mother, although she was raised in a convent and was very Catholic — she was forced to give up her Indian traditions. Don't feel that there's no hope, don't stop to think that there is no way that you can deal with the pain that you feel. I know what that pain is like, because I have felt it all my life. There are ways that you can deal with your pain, and the key to the solution is knowing what your people have done all their lives — they've survived for centuries. Yes, they've had to give up a lot of things but that knowledge is still in their hearts and in their minds, and you should be able to learn from that knowledge. Be proud of who you are, and if you don't know who you are — because a lot of us grow up that way — there are ways you can find out who you are. The more you find out about who you are, the more proud you will be and that will open up roads and paths for you to find your way through this. So it takes work on a spiritual level, it takes work on an intellectual level by studying, and it takes work on a physical level — you have to take care of your body, you have to keep it healthy.

—Inés Talamantez
Mescalero Apache

You need to think about the values and the lessons that are taught through the traditional stories. They teach us about being honest. They teach us not to steal, about being truthful and always being in control of our passions. A lot of those truths were told through the coyote stories and the coyote was used as an example of how not to be. A lot of bad things always happened to the coyote because of the wrong choices he made, doing the wrong thing. So we were taught what not to do, how not to be. We were also given stories using the wolf, who always emulated the good qualities and the opposite of the coyote. So we were taught values, we were taught good things through these stories. Many of these stories are passed along with our ceremonies.

—James Trosper
Shoshone/Arapaho

It's so important for each young person in North America to try and learn their own language. Like the Cree language; when you listen to it, there's no other language in the world that sounds like Cree. If you go to any country in the world, you will not hear that language. It is the same for Lakota, Apache, and the other Native languages; you don't hear them anywhere else in the world. When you hear our drum and our singing, our traditional music, you should know that there is no music anywhere in the world like ours. All of these are gifts from the Creator.

—Gordon Tootoosis
Cree

I look at how our people are living today and I think if we could just turn back to the traditional ways then our lives would be a lot better.

—James Trosper
Shoshone/Arapaho

Tribal and Spiritual Life

As the Keeper of the Sacred Pipe, as spiritual leader among our people, we have a great concern about the future generations. We have a lot of concerns about the cycle of life, because long ago my people used to live over 100 years, and today that has shortened way too much. Now the elders are much younger and by the time they get to 70 or 80 years old they've gone to the spirit world. According to our traditional lifestyle we're supposed to live 100 years or over, and today we're not making that. Our ways of life here on the earth are not good. People use a lot of foul language; people are in a lot of pain — spiritually, physically, mentally.

—Arvol Looking Horse
Lakota

There are many sacred ceremonies that are still alive. We have our Sun Dances; as far as I know all of the Plains tribes still have the Sun Dance, although they are done a little differently by each tribe. You can find those ceremonies. Present tobacco or a little offering to the elders and then find out more about the sacred ceremonies.

—Gordon Tootoosis
Cree

Nellie Menard, Lakota

Ben Marcus, Taos Pueblo

Fools Crow, Lakota

Haman Wise, Shoshone

The Sun Dance is a source of tremendous strength for our people. All across the high plains I see this tradition as being very strong and important for the way in which families carry out their lives. It weaves together several very important spiritual traditions: the Sweat Lodge, the medicine bundles, and the Vision Quest. The Sun Dance creates a very vibrant community that is dynamic; it's growing and people are very deeply involved in it — not only the elders but also people in their middle age and young people. I know in my family there are people as young as fifteen and twenty who are taking part in the Sun Dance as a year round spiritual expression.

The commitment that people in the Sun Dance give, the sacrifice they give on behalf of their families, is a great thing. A family member in a Sun Dance involves the entire extended family; so we see people saying, "Well, my auntie went into the Sun Dance because she was devoted to the health and well-being of her niece or nephew who's been ill, or to having her grandchildren in a good healthy home." That prayer, that expression, and that commitment of prayer, is very powerful. It focuses the whole family on the purpose of prayer. There are various gifts the sun dancers can have while they're in the Sun Dance Lodge, like the cattails, the mint, and the sage. Big family groups bring those gifts to the dancers to show respect and share prayers. The interaction of that many people with the Creator is a broad strengthening of the community — it's the talk of the town when there is a Sun Dance on: how many people went in and how long did they stay? All of that is very positive — it's an uplifting spiritual event in the community that is very, very important.

—Janine Pease
Crow/Hidatsa

When you make a commitment to go into the Sun Dance you make a vow to leave all of the outside world, to go into the Sun Dance Lodge and to pray to the Creator, to get closer to Him. When you sacrifice and you give up food and water, you enter a whole different realm — a whole different world. After the first full day of fasting it's like all the impurities have left your body and you're very humble; you become knowledgeable of how important the Creator is to you, and how dependent you are upon Him — through that ceremony you develop a close connection with the Creator.

In the Sun Dance we pray for the tribe, we pray for our country. Those prayers are really offered for all Indian people, for the whole world, and for the whole universe. We pray for everything. During the Sunrise Ceremony the leaders offer a special prayer and the purpose for that prayer is really a global prayer — we are praying for the whole world and really for the whole universe because everything in the Sun Dance represents a different part of the universe. That sunrise prayer and that time of the day are dedicated to the blessing of the whole world.

—James Trosper
Shoshone/Arapaho

Janine Pease, Crow/Hidatsa

Among Native peoples there is always a tribe somewhere that is praying for the livelihood of all the people, for their crops, for their harvest, their hunting, for a cure to sickness. Everybody is dancing and praying about these things. That's exactly what we do at our [Salish] wintertime ceremony, praying for this coming year, that we'll have a successful year. At the [Crow-Shoshone] Sun Dance they're carrying a heavy load, carrying some responsibility for their tribe — they're sacrificing these three days for themselves and all people. This is exactly what our tribe does in our wintertime ceremony; so in every tribe there is a ceremony that is being held for each season. This means that one tribe is not carrying the entire load for all the people. Every tribe has a time when they're praying for the world in general.

—John Arlee
Salish

Advice for Living in Two Worlds

In our American Indian communities, our children are surrounded by wonderful resources, right in your own home sometimes. There are people who know a great deal about our very own tribes, about our land, the language, about traditions. It is so important to learn about ways of living that have sustained our people for thousands of years. When I talk to my nieces and nephews and my grandchildren, I say, "Be daring, turn the TV off. Take a couple of days break from the cable TV and listen to your elders."

—Janine Pease
Crow/Hidatsa

We do have to live in today's world, we do have to learn the way that things work in to-day's world. But I don't think that we need to take the attitude of "out with the old, and in with the new." I think that we need to hold onto the old and we need to learn the new. This is important for our people. My advice to anybody is to hold onto the good things, to the old things that the Creator has taught to our people and that have passed down for generations.

—James Trosper
Shoshone/Arapaho

Sitting Bull said over 100 years ago, "Take the good and leave the bad." He was saying to the people that you should learn to go to school and get educated. We need to balance ourselves today through education, by going to school, and by also following our traditional way of life. We say that the mind, the body, and the spirit can bring wholeness to life — that is what we believe in. That is also why our ancestral language is important to know — at least be able to speak some words in your own language.

—Arvol Looking Horse
Lakota

What is paramount is attaining an education from the educational system from wherever we live, in my case here in Saskatchewan. The educational system is all in the English language so a person can make a living. That type of education teaches you how to make a living; but to know how to live you need a different learning. Our traditional background as First Nations people teaches us how to live. Both ways are important because to make a living we need schooling, but we must never forget the ways of our ancestors — that is the most important.

—Gordon Tootoosis
Cree

Austin Two Moons, Cheyenne

You need to exercise, you need to eat good healthy food, and you need to take care of your mind. The way you do that is by studying; even if you're not in school, you can read books and there's a lot you can learn from books. And there's also a lot you can learn from speaking with your elders, if you're in a situation where they are available to you. Begin to respect them because they have a lot of wisdom and they have the solution for us in terms of how to deal with society. You can be a member of this American society, because you are an American, but at the same time you are also a Native person and you can be a part of your Native culture. There are ways of doing that and one of the most important is by trying to learn the language.

—Inés Talamantez
Mescalero Apache

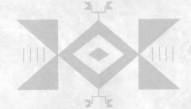

Our sacred way of life here is not good. Our Indian people suffer from a lot of different sicknesses, viruses, a lot of anger, hatred, a lot of foul language in our homes, and everything that we eat, the way we live in this very fast world — it's affecting us. But our ceremonies, our songs, our prayers are about life, about how sacred things are, and about trying to live a beautiful sacred way of life.

—Arvol Looking Horse
Lakota

There are so many ways in which our lives are filled with temptation to do dangerous things, to put our lives at risk, such as drugs, alcohol, and gambling. Those things are really harmful to each individual who is involved with them and to our community as a whole. While there are temptations, there are also ways to say "no" to all of that, to enjoy our culture, its music, and its dance.

There's a huge out of doors in almost all Indian country. Find out about our sacred places, where the battles were fought, where special events happened. The land is a beautiful place to be and there's so much of our nature to partake in. Become involved in ceremonies, know where the elders are, and be involved in prayer, in spiritual ways. These are the things that our Creator and our elders have given us, ways that make us strong.

—Janine Pease
Crow/Hidatsa

Take the time to be quiet and be by yourself and reflect on what your gifts are because there are two ways to go: you can go the good way and live in harmony with nature, which is what our ancestors have always done; or you can go the other way and end up in prison, because you didn't follow the good path, you followed the wrong path. Sometimes it seems as though it's easier to go the wrong path, because there are things out there that make you feel good, but it's only temporary. Those things don't make you feel good in your life, and what you need is to figure out what are the things that make you feel good. One of the things that makes you feel good is to get out into nature — go walking, go hiking, go swimming in the ocean, or wherever you live, in a river or a lake, experience the beauty of America, experience how America is such a sacred place. Everywhere you go in this land, our people have been there and they have said, "This place is sacred." We have to return to those ways by being in the natural world. Spend time hiking, walking, swimming, and being in the natural world; and recognize that our elders have always told us that we're connected to the natural world, that we have an obligation to it, to protect it.

—Inés Talamantez
Mescalero Apache

As an Indian young person, you should know that there are ways to take up your own identity just waiting for you. For example, if you think of the warrior tradition, they sought direction and vision, a very, very intimate relationship with the Creator, through the Sweat Lodge, the Vision Quest, and through the Sun Dance. All of these ways of spiritual expressions, all of that spiritual life, still exists today.

—Janine Pease
Crow/Hidatsa

I tell our youth, or anybody that needs help, that by turning back to our traditional ways, by turning back to the things that the Creator has blessed us with, we can find all the answers to all of the problems and all the challenges that we face today.

—James Trosper
Shoshone/Arapaho

Acbadadea, *Maker of All Things Above, hear my prayer. "I know it is important to explain the Indian religion to our youngsters, so they can know something about their heritage and traditional life, how it is different from other ways in which people live, especially in this modern world. Without this knowledge they do not have anything to fall back on, and I don't see how a person can live in this world without the center that is given by religion. They should know this, and respect the importance of prayer. For then they can have a basis upon which to decide whether to follow a path that You, The Maker of All Things Above, have set forth, or whether to wait for the consequences. This understanding is also important for non-Indians, for even though they have different religions, they can see that all religions are the same in their true meaning and that they all lead to You.*

Maker of All Things Above, I am thankful for what You have given me. As my life comes to a close, I realize that You have given me strength to stay with my prayers and even to be a leader of my religion. Just as You have given me the strength and words that will be put in this book, so, too, should You give understanding to those who read these words. This is my prayer. Aho! Aho!"

—Thomas Yellowtail
Crow

Thomas Yellowtail

BIOGRAPHICAL NOTES

JOE MEDICINE CROW is the Crow Tribal Historian and the oldest living man of the Crow tribe. In 1939, he was the first member of the Crow tribe to obtain a master's degree. Medicine Crow is the last traditional Crow chief, having achieved the war deeds necessary to be declared a "chief" during World War II. In 2009, he received the Presidential Medal of Freedom, the nation's highest civilian honor. Dr. Medicine Crow is a guest speaker at many colleges throughout the nation. His books include *A Handbook of Crow Indian Laws and Treaties*, *From the Heart of the Crow Country*, and *Counting Coup: Becoming a Crow Chief on the Reservation and Beyond*. He also wrote the Foreword to *All Our Relatives: Traditional Native American Thoughts about Nature* and *Custer's Last Battle: Red Hawk's Account of the Battle of the Little Bighorn* by Paul Goble. He lives on the Crow Reservation in Lodge Grass, Montana.

JANINE PEASE is the founding president of the Little Big Horn College in Crow Agency Montana, a past president of the American Indian Higher Education Consortium (for two terms), a director of the American Indian College Fund (for seven years), and was appointed by President Clinton to the National Advisory Council on Indian Education (for eight years). She wrote the Introductions for *Light on the Indian World: The Essential Writings of Charles Eastman (Ohiyesa)* and *The Spirit of Indian Women*. Dr. Pease has won several prestigious awards: National Indian Educator of the Year (1990), the MacArthur Fellowship Award (better known as the "Genius Award"), and the ACLU Jeanette Rankin Award. She has been named one of the "One Hundred Montanan's of the Century" by the *Missoulian Magazine*, a "Montanans to Remember" by *Montana Magazine*, and one of the fourteen most important American Indian leaders of the 20th century in *New Warriors*, by R. David Edmunds (University of Nebraska Press). She is also the recipient of Honorary Doctorate degrees from six different colleges and universities. Janine is a Crow and Hidatsa Indian, enrolled as a Crow. She is currently the Vice-President of Indian Affairs at Rocky Mountain College. She has two adult children and lives in Billings, Montana.

JAMES TROSPER is a Sun Dance chief of the Shoshone tribe on the Wind River Indian Reservation in Wyoming. He is from a long line of Shoshone Sun Dance chiefs that includes John Trehero, the Sun Dance chief who brought the Shoshone Sun Dance to the Crow tribe, and is a direct descendent of Chief Washakie, who is the most important chief of the Shoshone tribe in history. Mr. Trosper is deeply involved in developing and promoting programs to preserve the Shoshone language and cultural heritage. He is also part Arapaho, a director of the Chief Washakie Foundation, a director of the Grand Teton National Park Foundation, and a Trustee of the University of Wyoming. He wrote the Foreword for *Indian Spirit: Revised and Enlarged*. Trosper, his wife, and their two children, live in Fort Washakie, WY.

GORDON TOOTOOSIS, a veteran of over 40 films, appeared in *Reindeer Games* (2000) and *Legends of the Fall* (1994) with such actors as Brad Pitt and Anthony Hopkins. He has also acted in *Alaska* (1996) with Charlton Heston. Mr. Tootoosis won the Eagle Spirit Award at the American Indian Motion Picture awards in 2001. When Tootoosis became the guardian of his four grandchildren upon the untimely death of his daughter and son-in-law, he and his wife of over 40 years, Irene Seseequasis, moved from Los Angeles back to the Poundmaker Reserve in Saskatchewan Canada to raise their grandchildren. Tootoosis lived on the Poundmaker Reserve until his death in 2011.

JOHN ARLEE is a Salish traditional spiritual leader and teaches both the Salish language and Salish tribal history at the Salish Kootenai College in Pablo, MT. He is the author of *Over a Century of Moving to the Drum: Salish Indian Celebrations on the Flathead Reservation*. He has also recorded traditional songs on multiple CDs. He lives on the Salish Flathead Reservation in Arlee, Montana.

INÉS M. TALAMANTEZ is a professor at the University of California, Santa Barbara. Dr. Talamantez is a Mescalero Apache, a graduate of Dartmouth College, and the author of *Teaching Religion and Healing*. She has a book forthcoming on the Apache women's puberty ceremony and has contributed articles to *Native Religions and Cultures of North America: Anthropology of the Sacred* and *Unspoken Worlds: Women's Religious Lives*. She is the past president of the Indigenous Studies Group at the American Academy of Religion and is one of the most well known American Indian scholars. She has pioneered the creation of a PhD program in religious studies with an emphasis in Native American Religious Traditions at UCSB, awarding PhDs to twenty-six Native American scholars. She and her husband live in Santa Barbara.

ARVOL LOOKING HORSE is the 19th Generation Keeper of the original White Buffalo Calf Pipe, the sacred pipe of the Lakota, Dakota, and Nakota Nations. He is widely recognized as a chief and the spiritual leader of all three branches of the Sioux tribe. He is the author of *White Buffalo Teachings* and a guest columnist for *Indian Country Today*. A tireless advocate of maintaining traditional spiritual practices, Chief Looking Horse is the founder of Big Foot Riders, which memorializes the massacre of Big Foot's band at Wounded Knee, and World Peace Day. His prayers have opened numerous sessions of the United Nations and his many awards include the Juliet Hollister Award from the Temple of Understanding, a Non-Governmental Organization with Consultation Status with the United Nations Economic and Social Council. He lives on the Cheyenne River Reservation in South Dakota.

PHOTOGRAPHIC CREDITS

John Nicholas Choate: xiv, xv
Edward S. Curtis: xi, 66, 67, 68, 69, 70, 74, 75, 76, 77
Michael Grabner: 65
Åke Hultkrantz: 6, 11,14, 16, 17, 28, 29, 30, 31, 36, 38, 39, 48, 57, 59, 60, 61
Susana Marín: 84, 91
Fred E. Miller: x, xi, xii, xiii, xv
Richard Throssel: xvi, 82
William Wildschut: 54
85 photographs from the 1970s and 1980s Sun Dances as well 41 photographs of contemporary powwows and parades were taken by Michael Fitzgerald, 7 by Judith Fitzgerald, 6 by Dennis Sanders, and 5 by John Frost.

About Thomas Yellowtail

Born in 1903, medicine man and Sun Dance chief Thomas Yellowtail was the principal figure in the Crow-Shoshone Sun Dance Religion during the last half of the 20th century. As a youth he lived in the presence of old warriors, hunters, and medicine men who knew the freedom and sacred ways of pre-reservation life. In February 1993, when Yellowtail received the Montana Governor's Award for the Arts in recognition of his work in preserving the traditional culture of the Crow tribe, the program for the award ceremony contained the following quotation:

> This man is outside of time as we know it, centered in the spiritual world. Thomas Yellowtail has perpetuated the spiritual traditions of his Crow tribe as one of the last living links to pre-reservation days. But his legacy is not limited to Native Americans because his principles and his message benefit anyone searching to find a balance in this fast-paced technological society.

Yellowtail died at age 90 in 1993. He was one of the most admired American Indian spiritual leaders of the last century, although he was not the most prominent member of his immediate family. Historically, the Yellowtail family is the most famous Crow family of the 20th century. His older brother, Robert Yellowtail, was the first Native American superintendent of a reservation and was selected as Commissioner of Indian Affairs by President Eisenhower, although he declined the appointment. Yellowtail Dam and Yellowtail Reservoir in Montana are named after him. Susie Yellowtail, Thomas Yellowtail's wife, was the first Native American registered nurse, a tireless advocate of Native American issues, and is already enshrined in the Montana Hall of Fame in Helena, Montana. The many honors and awards that have been received by the Yellowtail family, including Thomas Yellowtail, are too numerous to mention.

The story of Yellowtail's life and his descriptions of the Sun Dance Religion are revealed in the book *Yellowtail: Crow Medicine Man and Sun Dance Chief*, edited by Michael Oren Fitzgerald. It was published by the University of Oklahoma Press (1991). Thomas Yellowtail also wrote the Introductions to *Indian Spirit*, edited by Michael and Judith Fitzgerald, and *The Feathered Sun*, by Frithjof Schuon.

About *Yellowtail: Crow Medicine Man and Sun Dance Chief*

As told to Michael Oren Fitzgerald
Introduction by Fred Voget

"As [Yellowtail] recounts his extraordinary personal experiences and defines the Crow religion, the magnitude of the loss to his people emerges along with wonder at his enduring faith and strength of spirit.... Important material for students investigating Native American history, anthropology, or religions."

—*Booklist Magazine*

"[Fitzgerald's] book becomes the personal testament of a pivotal figure in recent Crow cultural history. Fitzgerald examines the place of the Sun Dance, and of the sacred, in the life and future of the Crow.... It is a serious work of anthropology and history."

—*Choice Magazine*

"This new window onto the remarkable world of the Native American may be among the last that will be opened to us, for Yellowtail is one of the few remaining living links to that irreplaceable past. What is important is that this latest window is also one of our best.... The result is a compelling testament that may come in time to rival *Black Elk Speaks*."

—**Huston Smith**, University of California, Berkeley

"Authentic and conveying the character of Yellowtail's voice."

—*Publisher's Weekly*

About Michael Oren Fitzgerald

Michael Oren Fitzgerald has written and edited numerous publications on world religions, predominantly on American Indian spirituality. Four of his books on American Indian spirituality are used in college courses. Three of the books Fitzgerald has co-edited with his wife, Judith Fitzgerald, have received prestigious awards, including Best Book on Religion and Philosophy — 2005 by the Midwest Independent Publisher's Association for *The Spirit of Indian Women*. He holds a Doctor of Jurisprudence, cum laude, from Indiana University. Michael has taught Religious Traditions of North American Indians in the Indiana University Continuing Studies Department in Bloomington, Indiana. Fitzgerald has spent extended periods of time visiting traditional cultures and attending sacred ceremonies throughout the world, including the sacred rites of the Apsaroke, Sioux, Cheyenne, Shoshone, Bannock, and Apache tribes. He is an adopted son of the late Thomas Yellowtail, one of the most honored American Indian spiritual leaders of the last century, who also adopted Fitzgerald into the Crow tribe in 1971. He and his wife have an adult son and live in Bloomington, Indiana.

Michael and Judith Fitzgerald with Susie and Thomas Yellowtail, Bloomington, Indiana, 1980

"My son, Michael Fitzgerald, has been a member of my family and the Crow tribe for over twenty years. Michael has helped to preserve the spiritual tradition of the Crow Sun Dance and he has helped to show us the wisdom of the old-timers."
—Thomas Yellowtail

Books Written & Edited by Michael Oren Fitzgerald

Yellowtail: Crow Medicine Man and Sun Dance Chief, University of Oklahoma Press, 1991

The Essential Charles Eastman: Light on the Indian World, World Wisdom, 2002, Revised 2007
Silver Midwest Book Award for "Religion/Philosophy/Inspiration"

The Foundations of Christian Art: Illustrated, by Titus Burckhardt, World Wisdom, 2006
Gold Midwest Book Award for "Interior Layout"; Silver Benjamin Franklin Award for "Arts"

The Spiritual Legacy of the American Indian, by Joseph Epes Brown, World Wisdom, 2007

Introduction to Hindu Dharma: Illustrated, by HH the 68th Jagadguru of Kanchi, World Wisdom, 2008

Foundations of Oriental Art and Symbolism, by Titus Burckhardt, World Wisdom, 2009
Silver Midwest Book Award for "Illustration"

Living in Two Worlds: The American Indian Experience, by Charles Eastman, World Wisdom, 2010
Winner of the Foreword Magazine Book of the Year Gold Medal for "Social Science"; Winner of the Benjamin Franklin Gold Award for "Multicultural"; Midwest Book Award Golds for: "Culture," "Interior Layout," and "Color Cover"

Frithjof Schuon: Messenger of the Perennial Philosophy, World Wisdom, 2010

A King James Christmas: Biblical Selections with Illustrations from Around the World,
co-edited by Catherine Schuon, Wisdom Tales, 2012

Children of the Tipi: Life in the Buffalo Days, 2013

Books by Judith & Michael Oren Fitzgerald

Christian Spirit, World Wisdom, 2004
Gold Midwest Book Award for "Religion & Philosophy"

The Sermon of All Creation: Christians on Nature, World Wisdom, 2005
Silver Midwest Book Award for "Nature"; Silver Midwest Book Award for "Religion/Philosophy"

The Spirit of Indian Women, World Wisdom, 2005
Gold Midwest Book Award for "Multicultural"; Gold Midwest Book Award for "Religion/Philosophy"

The Universal Spirit of Islam, World Wisdom, 2006
Foreword Magazine Book of the Year Award Finalist for "Religion"; Silver Midwest Book Award for "Religion/Philosophy"
Silver Benjamin Franklin Award for "Religion"

Indian Spirit: Revised & Enlarged, World Wisdom, 2006
Gold Midwest Book Award for "Culture"; Gold Midwest Book Award for "Religion/Philosophy/Inspiration"

This double DVD set is a companion to the book
Native Spirit: The Sun Dance Way

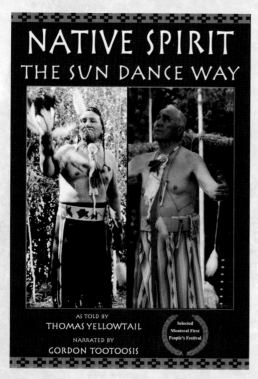

Official Selection at the *Montreal First Peoples' Festival, The American Indian Film Festival,* and *The Talking Stick Film Festival.*

The documentary film and more than two hours of Special Features include:

- the only known film footage of a Crow-Shoshone Sun Dance, taken in 1989;
- photographs from more than twenty Crow and Shoshone Sun Dances from 1903 to 2004;
- archival photographs of early reservation life;
- photographs of contemporary powwows and parades;
- film interviews with eight tribal elders from the Arapaho, Cree, Crow, Lakota, Mescalero Apache, Salish, and Shoshone tribes;
- original film interviews with Thomas Yellowtail;
- narration by Gordon Tootoosis.

Visit the Native Spirit website at
www.nativespiritinfo.com

This Internet site contains a teacher's guide for classroom use.

Free American Indian e-Products
Daily Inspirational Quotations

Judith and Michael Fitzgerald have selected many American Indian inspirational quotations and designed and created many patterns of American Indian e-stationery for use on the Internet. The quotations and e-stationery are combined to create "daily inspirational American Indian quotations" that can be automatically sent to readers each day via e-mail at no charge. Interested readers should visit the e-Products section of the publisher's Internet site at:

www.worldwisdom.com

Other Free American Indian e-Products

Judith Fitzgerald has also created American Indian wallpaper, screen savers, e-cards, and e-stationery that are available for no cost at the same website. New products are periodically added. World Wisdom provides all of these products to readers at no cost. The publisher and the editors hope these products will also provide a source of daily inspiration.